First-Place Reading

LEAP FORWARD

GRADE 3

⌒Harcourt

Orlando   Austin   Chicago   New York   Toronto   London   San Diego

Visit *The Learning Site!*
www.harcourtschool.com

ISBN 0-15-334557-8

2 3 4 5 6 7 8 9 10   039   10 09 08 07 06 05 04 03 02

CONTENTS

A Story for Pam

by **Sharon Fear**

illustrated by **Stephen Kellogg**

"Look at this ad," Teacher Dan said to the class. "It is an ad for a story."

The ad said, "Are you creative? Then write a creative story! See it in *Matt's Story Stack*."

"This ad will be homework, Class," said Teacher Dan. "I expect you to write a story. I will send it to *Matt's Story Stack*."

"How can I write a story?" Pam asked Teacher Dan. "What will I write?"

"What do you like, Pam? Do you like pets? You could write a pet story," suggested Teacher Dan.

"I had a pet crab," said Pam. "But it was sad to be a pet. Now my crab is in the sand. I can not write a pet story."

"Do you like flags, Pam? You could write a flag story," suggested Teacher Dan.

"I like flags," said Pam. "I have two flags. One flag is tan. It has a hat. One flag is black. It has a cat. But I have not researched flags. I can not write a flag story."

"Do you like to dance, Pam? You could write a dance story," suggested Teacher Dan.

"I like to dance," said Pam. "My dad is in the dance business. I can tap dance. I am not in the dance business. I can not write a dance story."

"You can write a story, Pam," said Teacher Dan. "You like pets. You like flags. You like to dance. You are a responsible cat. You can write a story for Matt the Cat.

Pam was sad. She sat and sat. "I can not write a story," she said. "I like pets. I like flags. I like to dance. But I can not write a creative story."

Then Pam sat up. Now she was glad. "I CAN write a story!" Pam said. "I like pets. I like flags. I like to dance. I am responsible. I will write a creative Pam story for homework! My Pam story will be in *Matt's Story Stack!* That is all there is to that!"

Think About It

1. How does Teacher Dan help Pam with her story?

2. Why do you think Pam will write a Pam story?

3. What will Pam write in her story? Think about what Pam likes. Then write the story.

Prefixes and Suffixes

Pam writes **nonstop**. *Nonstop* has two parts: *non* and *stop*. A **prefix** is a word part that is added to the beginning of a word. A **suffix** is a word part that is added to the end of a word. Prefixes and suffixes can change the meanings of base words.

Prefixes	Suffixes
dis- ("not") non- ("not") over- ("over")	-able ("able to be") -tion ("the act of") -ion ("the act of")

Knowing about word parts can help you read new words. Find a word with a prefix or a suffix in each sentence. What does the new word mean?

When I run, I run nonstop.

My story has a likable cat in it.

Add the prefix or suffix to the base word. Write a sentence with the new word.

over- look	act -ion	stack -able

My Week at Camp Wonder

by Deborah Eaton
illustrated by Howard Weliver

Mom,

    I like everyone at summer camp a lot.
Look what I got! It likes to get in my suitcase.
It is <u>not</u> poisonous. Doc Ross said so when it
bit Counselor Bob.

                   Todd

Mom,

    My sock can hop! Look at this! It could win medals for hopping. What makes it hop? Something is in the sock. It is a frog! A friend got the frog in there. Now there is a big spot on it. Will you get the spots out?

                        Todd

Mom,

    I did something to my suitcase. It had all my rocks in it. Now it has a rip in it. Do not get mad!
I can fix it. See?

Todd

Mom,

I lost my harmonica in the pond. I practiced as I sat on a big rock. Then Counselor Bob said, "STOP!" And DROP! I lost it. Everyone cheered. They like my songs a lot.

Todd, the Summer
Camp Kid

Mom,

    I have something in my cabin. It's a dog! He got on my cot. Then everyone ran. It was odd! He looks like a hotdog. He's my friend. Mom, may I have him? He can sit in my suitcase. Ask Pop!

             Todd

Todd,

    You have to come back now. This box is for the hotdog dog. Get him in it for the trip back. We miss you, summer camp kid!

                    Mom

Think About It

1. Does Todd have fun at camp? How can you tell?

2. Why does everyone run out of Todd's cabin when the hotdog dog gets onto his cot?

3. Write a letter from Todd to Counselor Bob. Tell what happened when he got home with his new pet.

Predict Outcomes

When you read this story, did you wonder what was going to happen to Todd next? You can **make predictions**. You can think about the story facts and what you know from life. You can put those things together to make a prediction.

This web shows how you can predict what will happen in "My Week at Camp Wonder."

Fact in the Story
Todd asks his mom if he can have a pet.

What I Know
Moms want kids to be happy.

Prediction
Todd will get to take the pet home.

Making predictions can help you be a better reader. Reread page 17. Then use a web to help you make a prediction. What will happen when Todd and his new pet get off the bus?

Justin and Jessica

written by
Susan McCloskey

illustrated by
Mark Bixby

Justin looked at his desk.

"Letters, letters, letters!" he said.
"Hundreds to collect and send out. One for
the police department. One for the dance
teacher. One for the students in Miss Drum's
class. Who will get the letters there?"

"Not Ron Summs. He had an accident. He dropped a cup. He cut his hand. Not Pat Plums. She fell in the tub. She bumped her leg. That makes two accidents. Not Gil Grumps. He tripped on a rug."

Justin's expression was sad. "Who will help?" he asked.

Just then, who did he see? Jessica!
She was looking for a job.

Justin said, "You are just the one I'm
looking for. I have hundreds of letters to
get out. Can you do it, Jessica?" Jessica
jumped up and down. Yes, she could!

"Go for it, Jessica!" said Justin. "This is a rush job. I wish you luck."

Jessica obeys commands, so she went fast.

Everyone looked at her. They laughed and grinned. It was fun for Jessica.

Jessica did a winning job. The letter to the police department got there. The letter to the dance teacher got there. Best of all, the letter to the students in Miss Drum's class got there.

A bunch of the kids jumped up to see Jessica. One kid hugged her! They begged her to come back and visit.

Jessica did visit. Justin went with her. The audience clapped and clapped.

"Speech, speech!" they said.

Speech? Not from Jessica.

But Justin said it all for her—with a big grin.

Think About It

1. How do the letters get sent out?

2. Why does Jessica not make a speech?

3. Suppose the TV news wants a story about Jessica. Write the TV news story.

Story Elements

Justin and Jessica live in a small town. They have to get lots of letters out on time. These are the most important parts of this story.

Every story has three parts, or elements. The **setting** is the time and place in which the story happens. The **characters** are the people and animals in the story. The **plot** is what happens in the story.

The story map below tells about "Justin and Jessica."

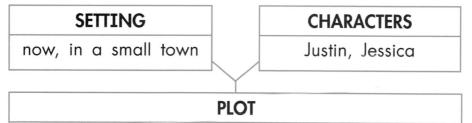

SETTING	CHARACTERS
now, in a small town	Justin, Jessica

PLOT
Justin has to have help getting the letters out. Jessica, a kangaroo, does a good job of helping.

Plan a story of your own. On a sheet of paper, make a story map like the one above to show your plan.

CREATURE CLICKS

by Kana Riley

All children like to watch creatures. Some adults do this as a job. They get photos that let us see how creatures survive.

Getting the photos can be hard for them. It has to be something they like to do. Just look at some of the spots they had to go to!

Marine Creatures

This sub went far down in the sea to get this shot. It is so dark, that this part of the sea looks black.

Without the sun, some marine creatures still survive. Fish and crabs like the sea bottom.

The creatures there are odd. Notice how delicate some look. This spot could kill us, yet they dart and swim there without harm.

Yard Creatures

You may not have noticed some of the bugs in the yard and in the park. Are you curious? Look at what is out there!

This smart bug looks like an ant. Some friends with feathers can not tell the two apart. They do not like an ant for a snack. So they do not harm this bug. It can survive well in the yard.

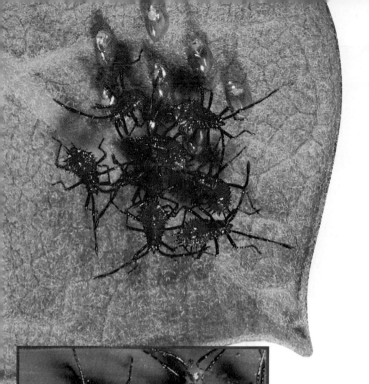

Some mom bugs park next to eggs to see them hatch. Some moms are not curious. They go off to do what they like.

This dad bug has all the eggs stuck on his back. So far he has not collapsed! It can be hard to be a bug!

Think About It

1. Where and how do the creatures in this selection live and survive?

2. How do the photos help you learn about creatures you may not have seen on your own?

3. If you could be any creature you liked, what would you choose to be? Write a paragraph explaining your choice and telling what life would be like as that creature.

Vocabulary in Context

In "Creature Clicks" you may have come to a new word you could sound out but not understand. Sometimes other words and sentences, or the **context**, can tell you what the word means.

Reread these sentences from "Creature Clicks."

This dad bug has all the eggs stuck on his back. So far he has not collapsed!

The words in the first sentence help you know that *collapsed* means "fallen down."

Now read this sentence from the first part of "Creature Clicks." What other words help you know what *marine* means?

It is so dark that this part of the sea looks black. Without the sun, some marine creatures still survive.

A NEW BEST FRIEND

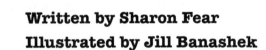

Written by Sharon Fear
Illustrated by Jill Banashek

"Write to me!" Howard shouted.

"I will!" Rick shouted back. The car and the moving van started off. They went down the block, around the playground, and beyond it.

Rick was moving to a new town.

"I wish I could go, too," Howard said to his friend Beth.

"Will you be lonely without him?" asked Beth.

"He was my BEST friend," Howard said seriously.

"Help me with my kite," said Beth. Howard held the kite. Beth unwound some string. She fastened the string to the kite.

"You can get a new best friend," said Beth. Howard frowned. "How? Who?"

Howard's dog bounded up to them. Beth picked up a stick and tossed it. "Get it, Bow Wow!" Beth shouted.

"How about Jack?" she asked.

"Jack does not like Bow Wow," Howard said.

"How about Norman?" said Beth.

"Norman who?" asked Howard.

"His dad has a brown mustache," said Beth.

"Bow Wow does not like Norman," said Howard.

Bow Wow growled.

"See," said Howard.

Howard picked up his basketball, dribbled it, and shot. It rimmed around and fell out. He passed it to Beth. She dribbled around him. She shot. Pow! She sank it!

"Wow!" shouted Howard. "Outstanding!"

"I have a secret gift," teased Beth. They played on trading shots.

"Chuck!" she said. "Chuck could be your new best friend."

Howard frowned. "Chuck can't play basketball," he said. "Not like you."

"How about Ben?" said Beth.
"Can't swim," said Howard.
"Patrick?" said Beth.
"Can't play chess," said Howard.
"Carl!" shouted Beth.
"Can't do a cartwheel," said Howard.
"I give up," said Beth, doing a cartwheel.

Then it came to him. Beth was his friend. She was a girl, but she was the best.

"How about you?" Howard said.

She looked at him. "Can you dribble with your left hand?" she teased again.

"Yes," said Howard.

"You wish!" She laughed out loud. "Well, let's work on it now." She passed him the basketball.

"Outstanding!" said Howard.

Think About It

1. Why is Howard looking for a new best friend? Who will be his best friend now?

2. Why does it take Howard so long to know who his new best friend will be?

3. Howard is going to write to Rick. What do you think he will say? Write a letter for Howard to send.

Synonyms and Antonyms

When Beth makes a good shot, Howard tells her it is *outstanding*. The author could have used another word that means the same thing.

Synonyms are words that have almost the same meaning. **Antonyms** are words that have opposite meanings.

This chart shows a synonym and an antonym for a story word from "A New Best Friend."

Synonym	Story Word	Antonym
She was the **greatest.**	She was the **best.**	She was the **worst.**

Authors pick words that help describe what they are writing about. Readers look for clues in the author's words to help them understand new words and ideas.

Think about something you can describe. Write a sentence. Next, rewrite the sentence using a synonym and then an antonym. How does the meaning change?

That tree is _____.

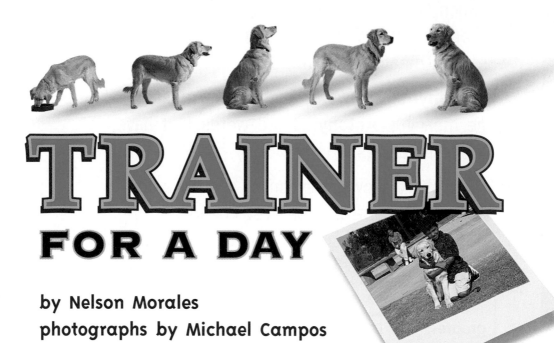

TRAINER
FOR A DAY

by Nelson Morales
photographs by Michael Campos

Here I am with our special pup, Jake. That's my sister Janet on the bench.

Jake is Janet's dog for now. Mom, Dad, and I all play with Jake and have lots of fun with him. We work hard on Jake's training, too.

Jake is going to be a working dog. He will help someone who can't see.

Jake will be a good working dog. He is very gentle. He likes everyone, and he can cheer anyone up! He is very smart, too. After his training, he will have lots of important skills for his work.

Janet and Jake are part of a special program. In this program, kids can help train a working dog. When the training is over, Janet will have to give Jake up. That will be hard for all of us. Still, we are all glad to know that Jake will be helping someone.

Jake has to be comfortable anywhere he is taken. That's why Mom and Dad take Jake to work now and then. We take him to shops and parks. He comes with me when I have an appointment with the doctor. Wherever we go, Jake can go. It's part of his training.

Jake likes to go on car trips. He likes to go on the bus, too. All these trips will help Jake know how to be a good working dog.

Dad and I like to watch the planes take off and land. Jake comes with us. He sits still and watches the planes. I wish I could know what Jake is thinking!

Mom, Dad, Janet, and I are going to take a plane trip. Jake will come with us. That trip will be one of the best parts of training Jake.

When I got to take Jake to class, Janet had to tell me what to do. "One skill Jake has to have is to be calm when someone approaches him. Be firm and confident when you tell him what to do. Do not forget to let him know when he is doing a good job."

Janet had a lot to say! At last, Jake and I were off.

When we got there, Jake and I went into the playground. Lots of kids were playing on the equipment. They jumped down and rushed over to see Jake.

To some of the kids I said, "Do not approach Jake too fast. Do not yell at him."

To some I said, "It's all right. Jake is a very gentle dog."

Jake let all the kids pet him. "Good dog, Jake," I said.

Jake's training is going well. Maybe I will be the next one to have a special pup like Jake.

Think About It

1. Why does Janet work hard to train Jake?

2. Why is going lots of places part of Jake's training?

3. If you were Jake's trainer for a day, what would you do? Make a plan for the day. Tell why you would do each thing.

Main Idea

Jake is in training to be a working dog. That is the **main idea** in "Trainer for a Day." The main idea is the message the author wants to tell. To find the main idea, ask yourself, "What is this selection mostly about?"

In the web below, the main idea is in the center circle. The other sentences tell more about the main idea. Find the main idea in the paragraph.

Jake will be a good working dog. He is very gentle. He likes everyone, and he can cheer anyone up. He is very smart, too.

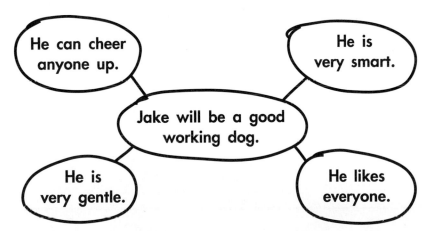

Sometimes the author states the main idea in a sentence. Sometimes readers have to figure it out on their own. Read a paragraph in a science textbook. Can you find the main idea?

Many Moons Ago

by Diane Hoyt-Goldsmith
illustrated by Franklin Ayers

Many moons ago, in the far north, it was dark all the time. This was because the sun, the moon, and the stars were hidden in three bags. The bags hung inside a mean man's house.

At that time, animals were very clever. They could sing and tell stories. Some could play tricks on those who were around.

Raven was one skillful creature. He could go as swiftly as an arrow over the land. Gazing down, he could see things happen from miles away.

Like all the rest of the animals, Raven was tired of the dark. He had a plan.

The mean man had a wife but no children. One time the wife was outside. Something made a tiny sound. "Gah! Gah!" it cried. She looked around and found a baby, all alone. She did not know the baby was Raven.

"Look," she said to the man. "I have found a baby who needs us." Then she made a big feast. She wanted to feed the baby. "Eat this," she said. "It's good for you."

Raven would not eat. All he would do was say
"Gah! Gah! Gah!" He got louder and louder and louder.

The wife was sad. "What can we do?" she asked
the man. "Our little baby will not eat."

"Maybe he wants a plaything," said the man. He
looked at the three bags. He got down the bag with
the stars and gave it to Raven. Raven stopped making
his sounds and smiled.

Then Raven opened the bag. The stars tumbled out,
and up they went. They arranged themselves into
twinkling pictures of animals.

Raven smiled a little. Then he started to make his sounds again. "Gah! Gah! Gah!"

"Give him more things," said the wife. The man gave Raven the bag with the moon. When Raven opened the top, out came the moon. It rose over the canyon and lit up the dark. "Gah!" said Raven.

"No more playthings for you!" the man said.

When they were all in bed, Raven made more loud sounds. The wife was sad. The man tossed and turned. He could not sleep. "Gah! Gah! Gah!" Raven cried.

The man got down the last bag. He gave it to Raven. When Raven opened the bag, out came the sun, red and hot.

Up, up, up rose the sun. It lit up the deepest canyons and the darkest forests. All the animals could feel its heat.

Clever Raven shed his costume and showed what he was. "Gah!" he shouted with pride.

He still has not stopped. Even now you can hear him calling, "Gah! Gah! Gah!"

Think About It

1. How does Raven make the world different?

2. Why do you think Raven will not eat any of the feast the wife made?

3. How does the world look before Raven lets out the stars, the moon, and the sun? How does it look afterward? Draw two pictures. Write sentences to go with your pictures.

Sequence

Raven gets the stars, the moon, and the sun from the mean man. This story tells about these events in time order, or **sequence**. Often writers use time-order words to show the order in which things happen.

first	next	then	later	finally

This chart shows the order of some events from "Many Moons Ago."

First, the woman finds the baby and brings him home.

↓

Next, she cooks a big feast, but the baby won't eat.

↓

Then the baby cries and cries.

↓

The man gives the baby his bag with the stars.

Think about the other events in "Many Moons Ago." What happens next? What is the last thing that happens in the story?

Plan your own story about something Raven does. Think about the events in your story. Draw a chart like the one above to show those events in time order.

This Is My Story

by Diane Hoyt-Goldsmith
photographs by Lawrence Migdale

When I was a girl, I loved to read. If my mother needed me, she could find me sprawled on my bed reading. My favorite stories were about faraway lands or other times.

I loved art, too. I drew and painted and cut and glued. I worked hard to perfect each picture. When I entered an art contest, I was a winner! Then I wanted to be an artist.

When I grew up, I made a career of my two favorite things. I became an artist and a writer. For many years, I worked in New York, publishing stories for children. I worked with an editor. We chose the art and the photos.

The title of the first story I wrote is *Totem Pole*. It tells how David and his father make a totem pole.

To write this story, I went to visit David in the state of Washington. I found out many new things in the time I spent there. I watched as the totem pole was made. David's family and friends told me folktales. They were fine retellers of these old stories.

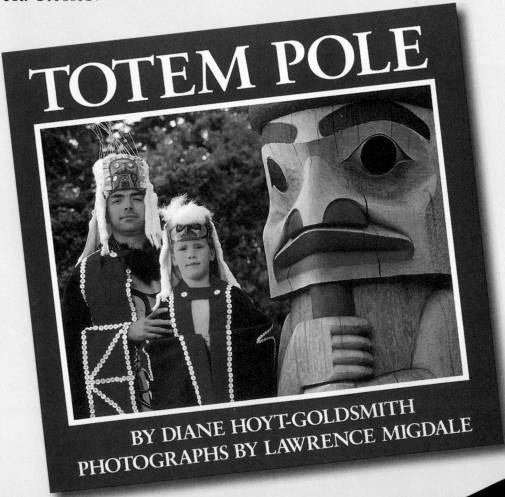

TOTEM POLE

BY DIANE HOYT-GOLDSMITH
PHOTOGRAPHS BY LAWRENCE MIGDALE

For a true story, an author must get all the facts. I used a tape recorder when I spoke with David. I also wrote many notes. My notes and the tape recordings helped me remember what I found out.

My friend Mr. Migdale did the photos of David and the totem pole. I used these pictures so readers could see what I wrote about. I wrote the story so others could see how totem poles are made.

When I wrote the story, I used a computer.
That way I could correct mistakes with ease.
I had to revise my writing many times before
I was finished.

My first published story was a success!
Many children liked to read about David and
the totem pole.

Now I am the author of many true stories.
I make it a rule to tell about real children and
real things.

Each time I start a new story, I go somewhere different. In my career as an author, I have traveled more than 100,000 miles. I have made new friends in many states.

As a girl, I traveled far and wide by reading. Now my stories help children do the same. Now I travel for real and do all the things I used to dream about!

Think About It

1. What did the author have to do to write her first book?

2. Why do you think the author writes true stories?

3. Write a letter to the author of "This Is My Story." Tell her what you liked most about her story.

ARCTIC HUNTER
BY DIANE HOYT-G
PHOTOGRAPHS BY LAV

PUEBLO STORYTELLER
BY DIANE HOYT-GOLDSMITH
PHOTOGRAPHS BY LAWRENCE MIGDALE

Fact and Opinion

In "This Is My Story" there are many facts about the author's life. Sometimes writers also give their opinions about things. A **fact** is a statement that can be checked. An **opinion** tells what someone thinks or feels.

Fact or Opinion?

Is It a Fact?	Is It an Opinion?
Can it be checked? Could someone show that it is true?	Does it tell someone's feelings? Does the writer use words that show feelings, such as *good* or *bad*?
Example I worked with an editor.	**Example** They were fine retellers of these old stories.

It is important for readers to be able to tell a fact from an opinion. Readers can then form their own ideas about what they read.

Read these sentences. Which is a fact and which is an opinion?

I became an artist and a writer.

The best stories are about faraway lands or other times.

Auction Day

by Carol Storment
illustrated by Anthony Carnabuci

When Ty spied the pony in the pen of wild horses, he knew what he had to do. First he went to the bank.

"How much money do I have?" he asked.

The man smiled. "You're a rich man, Tyrone. You have six dollars."

"Is that enough for that pony outside?" asked Ty.

The man looked out the window. "Oh no, Ty. Those horses will go for ten dollars or more. Besides, what good would a wild pony be on a farm?"

Ty didn't say another word. He went across the road to the store. Ty had a plan to get his pony.

"Is there any work I could do for you, Mrs. Wyman?" Ty asked. "I need some extra money."

The storekeeper said, "Why yes, Tyrone. I'll find something for you to do."

Ty started by sweeping up. All morning he worked around the store, stacking shelves and cleaning the back room. When he was done, Mrs. Wyman gave him a dollar.

Ty walked by the pen full of wild horses. There she was, the littlest pony. Her coat was so black, it was almost blue. "Hello, Blue Sky," Ty said. He put out his hand. The shy pony jumped away. Her eyes were wild, but they looked sad, too.

"Be brave, girl!" Ty said. "You'll be out of here tomorrow."

The next day, Ty went to see three of his neighbors. He asked each one, "Is there work I can do for you?"

"You bet there is!" they all said.

First, Ty cut tall grass for Mr. Dyer. Then he moved a pile of rocks for Mr. Ryan. He fed chickens and collected eggs for Mrs. Bly. He worked until Mrs. Bly fried some eggs for his lunch. She asked Ty what he needed the money for.

"A pony" was all he would say. Then he went back to work. Ty tried his best to do each task well. He wanted his neighbors to be satisfied with his work.

When Ty was done, each neighbor was happy
and paid him one dollar. Now he had three more
dollars! The neighbors watched as he left for
home. "That Tyrone works hard," they all agreed.
"But he'll have his hands full if he tries to tame a
wild pony!"

When Ty got home, he got out his bank. He
counted all his money. Then he borrowed a horse
and rode as fast as he could into town. He ran to
the bank. It was still open.

"I'll take my six dollars, please," Ty told the
man.

The man smiled. "Here you go. Good luck at the
sale tomorrow!"

The sale started early. Everyone in the county came to see the wild horses. Ty was there with his money clutched in his hand.

The auctioneer called out that it was time to start. The bids began. The horses were going for much more than ten dollars. Ty felt like crying. He wouldn't have enough money!

At last only Blue Sky was left. Ty bid ten dollars. Everyone in town knew how much Ty wanted that pony. No one said a word.

"Sold!" shouted the auctioneer. "That pony is all yours, son."

All of Ty's neighbors clapped for him.

Ty and his family got Blue Sky home and into her new pen. Ty sat and watched her for a while. Her blue-black coat was glistening in the sun. Her mane was flying in the wind. But her eyes were still wild and sad. Then Ty got up and opened the gate. Blue Sky shot out and galloped away.

His father ran up. "Ty! Why did you let the pony get away? You worked so hard to get the money for her!"

Ty said, "Blue Sky would never be happy living on a farm. I was glad to spend my money to set her free."

Ty felt proud as his pony galloped to freedom. *Fly away, Blue Sky!*

Think About It

1. What does Ty do so that he can buy Blue Sky?

2. Why do you think Ty doesn't tell anyone he plans to set Blue Sky free?

3. Write the diary entry Ty might write the day he lets Blue Sky go.

Characters' Feelings and Actions

Ty sets Blue Sky free because he feels sorry for the sad-looking pony. The way story characters act can show you how they feel.

To know how a character feels, think about what the character says and does. Look for words the author or other characters use to describe him or her.

This chart shows what Ty does when the auction is about to start. It shows his feelings, too.

Action	Feeling
clutches his money in his hand	worried about the auction

On a sheet of paper, chart a story character's actions and feelings. List some actions from another story you know, and then write the feeling each one shows you.

Action	Feeling

Action	Feeling

HARVEST TIME

by Sydnie Meltzer Kleinhenz
illustrated by Cheryl Kirk Noll

"It's harvest time, Lizzie," Dad said.

Mom said, "How about a harvest party tomorrow?"

I clapped my hands. Dad nodded. "Everybody bring a memory-maker," he called as he hurried off to work.

We don't always get a harvest from our banana trees. Bananas grow well in the tropics, but we live on Galveston Island. Sometimes the Texas winter is too cold for banana plants. Sometimes a tropical storm blows off the flowers. Then no fruit can grow. The years we do get bananas, we have a harvest party.

76

On Saturday morning I went to the trading market. I was looking for a memory-maker. At last I found the perfect thing—a tiny plastic sailing schooner. It was a bargain, so I got it and ran home.

First, I glued the little ship on the inside of a jar lid. Next, I put glitter and water in the jar. Last, I put on the lid and taped around it. I finished the memory-maker just as Dad called, "Harvest time, party time!"

We all met on a blanket on the grass. When I looked up, it seemed as if the banana leaves reached as high as the sky. Some of the bananas were still green. Some were as yellow as the bus I ride each day.

Dad put my spelling folder on the blanket. "Here is my memory-maker," he said. "I'm thankful to my Grandma and Grandpa Jakoby. When they came to America, they studied hard to speak English. That helped them find good jobs and get this fine house."

Spelling

Mom's memory-maker was a mixing bowl. "I'm thankful that Grandma and Grandpa Jakoby planted bananas. Now we can eat them as snacks or bake tasty treats with them."

I turned my memory-maker upside down and gave it a shake. The glitter looked like swirly snow around the ship.

"I'm thankful that Dad's Grandma and Grandpa Jakoby left their cold and snowy home. I'm glad the ship sailed safely to Galveston Island. I like living where it's mostly warm and sunny."

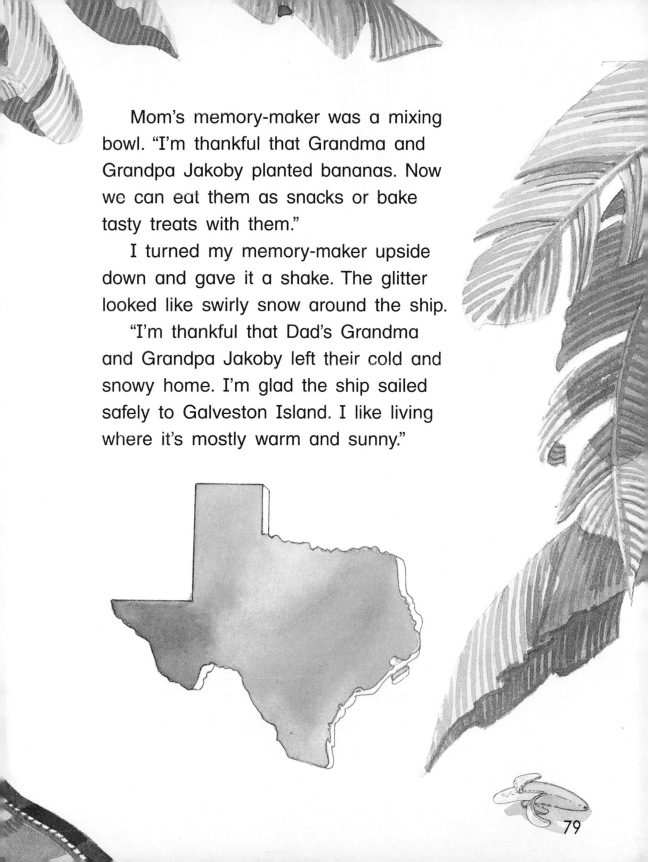

Mom gave me a squeeze. "You're not the only one who likes it sunny," she said.

Dad told the rest of our family story. Then he got his machete and said, "Let's cut bananas."

Mom and I helped support the bunch as Dad cut the stem. It felt as if we were holding a big log up in the air! My arms were rubbery when we softly set the bananas on the blanket.

We packed small bunches of bananas in bags and carried them to our neighbors. Then it was party time!

First we broke bananas into the blender. Mom added milk, Dad added sweetener, and I added ice. Dad hit the button to whir the mix into milkshakes. The river of banana foam felt frosty all the way down to my belly! We put the extra drink mix into molds to freeze solid. We would have banana ice pops for later.

After that, we mashed bananas to a pulp. We made pans and pans of banana muffins. Some were to give away. Some were to freeze and save. We nibbled banana muffins as we cleaned up.

I filled up on plenty of banana treats. And we all made plenty of memories to last until next harvest time.

Think About It

1. Why does the family bring memory-makers to the harvest party?

2. How often do Lizzie and her mom and dad have a harvest party? How do you know?

3. The next time they get bananas, Lizzie invites other family members to the harvest party. Make the invitation she sends. Use words and pictures in the invitation.

Summarize

Lizzie's dad tells the family story at the harvest party. To **summarize** the story, Lizzie would tell just the most important things that happen.

A story summary is much shorter than the story. The events are told in order and in your own words.

Read the sentences in the box. They give a summary of "Harvest Time."

> It was time to have a harvest party.
>
> Lizzie, her dad, and her mom shared their memory-makers.
>
> Then they harvested the bananas and took some to their neighbors.
>
> The family made banana treats.

Now read these sentences. Tell why each sentence doesn't belong in a summary of "Harvest Time."

Some Texas winters are too cold for banana plants.
Lizzie found the plastic schooner at the market.

Think about a story you know. What are the most important things that happen? Write a summary of the story.

BOOK OF DAYS

written by
Deborah Akers

illustrated by
Mercedes McDonald

Date: April 2

Dear Sue,

I felt so blue after you drove away! Now I have a plan. I will keep each day in this book until my big sister is home again. Then you can read about everything you missed, and I will feel less lonely.

I put myself in charge of your flower box. There were three new green sprouts in the soil. You said there would soon be a rainbow of flowers. I poured a little more water to hurry them along. I could tell they wondered where you were.

Date: April 6

Dear Sue,

Today was a good day. We worked in the garden, and Mom put me in charge of the carrot seeds. I pushed them into the dirt the way you showed me.

Remember last fall, when we dug beds for the plants to sleep in? Most of them are still sleeping, but a few seem to be stirring. The sweet pea sprouts are reaching for the sun with soft, curly fingers.

Date: April 9

Dear Sue,

Today I put myself in charge of the fruit trees. I walked down every row, and counted all the trees that have buds.

Here is a branch from the apple tree. Remember when we picked a basketful of apples? Then you helped me bake my first pie. I felt like a real cook!

The trees seem as if they are holding secrets in their tight buds. I think they are waiting for the right person to share them with. I know just how they feel.

Date: April 13

Dear Sue,

Today was an average day. While Mom went into town, Dad and I walked down to the river. I collected rocks for you on the beach. There were lots of beautiful ones, but I was choosy. I took just a few you could put on your desk.

Guess what happened next? I saw tracks in the sand! Our friend the fox is back, with some baby foxes, too. That must mean spring is really here. When will you be home? You're missing everything!

Date: April 21

Dear Sue,

Today the sky could not stop crying, and your flower box was swimming in rain. I watched from the porch as pools grew in the garden. The fruit trees shook in the storm.

A good thing happened today, too—there was a rainbow. I remembered the special rainbow wish we always make when it rains. I made my wish. Mom said she had a feeling it would come true soon.

Date: April 22

Dear Sue,

   Mom was right! I woke up to a sunny
day and ran outside. I think the garden
must have heard a signal in the night. There
were leaves and blooms and little celebrations
everywhere!

   Then came the best news! You are coming
home tonight! Now I am putting myself in
charge of the biggest celebration of all!

Think About It

1. Why does the girl write in her book of days? What does she write about?

2. Do you think the girl in the story will go on writing in her book of days? Tell why you think as you do.

3. Imagine that a friend or family member is out of town. Write a journal entry for a special day you would want him or her to know about.

Important Details

The main character in "Book of Days" writes letters to help her feel less lonely while her sister is away. The author gives details that tell you more about this main idea. **Details** answer questions like these:

Who?   *What?*   *Where?*

When?   *How?*   *Why?*

Here is a web that shows a main idea and some details.

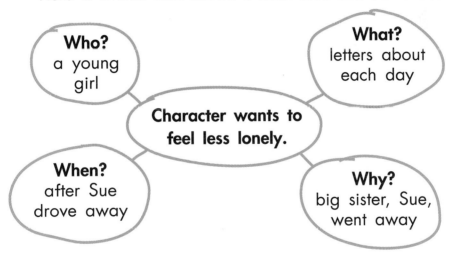

Each of the girl's letters to her sister has a main idea and some details. Choose one letter, and make a web like the one shown. Show at least three details that give more information about the main idea.

A MOUNTAIN
BLOWS ITS TOP

A chain of mountains runs along the west coast of North America. It's called the Cascade Range.

The mountains in this range are beautiful. Visitors hike and camp there. Loggers cut trees for lumber. Birds and animals make their homes in the forests, fields, and rivers.

STORY BY KANA RILEY

These peaks were formed long ago by volcanoes. Deep in the center of our planet is hot melted rock called magma. On top of it float plates of hard rock that form the planet's crust.

In 1980 the plates under the Cascade Range started to shift. The edges of the plates pushed up magma. As the magma rose, it caused the north side of Mount St. Helens to bulge. It made the ground shake. Plumes of steam began to shoot out of the old crater, or hole, at the top. Was the mountain ready to blow? No one knew.

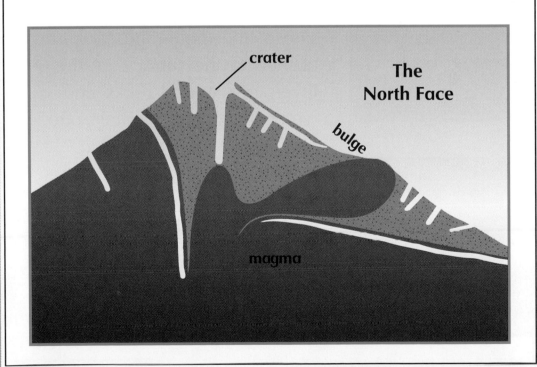

Sunday, May 18, 1980, dawned clear. Snowcapped Mount St. Helens caught the early rays of the sun. All seemed peaceful.

Then suddenly, at 8:32 A.M., the ground began to shake. The epicenter of this quake was very near Mount St. Helens.

This was a big one! With a mighty blast, it cracked the side of the mountain. Magma gushed to the surface, pushing layers of dirt and rocks and water in front of it. Blast after blast rocked the mountain.

Blocks of ice went flying. Water turned to steam. Rocks exploded into dust. Hot ash flew 12 miles into the sky.

Yakima, Washington, is 85 miles from Mount St. Helens. By 9:30 A.M. the sky in Yakima began to grow black. Lightning flashed. It looked as if a storm were coming.

But it was not rain that fell. It was ash. The tiny bits had edges as sharp as glass. They hurt everyone's eyes and made it hard to breathe.

All day ash fell. Soon every surface was covered with layers of it. Workers later swept up more than 600,000 tons from the streets and buildings.

When the big blasts stopped, Mount St. Helens was an awesome sight. The top of the mountain was not there. In its place was a huge, gray hole. From the center of it, clouds of ash still puffed into the air.

The land around the mountain looked like the surface of the moon. All was still. Trees were spilled all over the ground like match sticks. Rivers were choked with mud. Most of the animals had been caught by the blasts. No birds sang.

It has been many years since the mountain blew. What has Mount St. Helens taught us?

It has taught us that our planet is always changing. The blast showed us the awesome damage these changes can cause.

Yet we also saw that in time the land will heal. New plants now grow out of the layers of ash. Animals have come back. The rivers run clear once more.

What's going on inside the mountain? It's not quiet yet. In the center of the crater, another dome of magma is growing. Sometimes steam and ash gush out of it. They help us remember that our planet is still alive and still shaking.

Think About It

1. What happened when Mount St. Helens erupted? What has happened since then?

2. Will Mount St. Helens erupt again? What makes you think as you do?

3. Think about life in Yakima on the day Mount St. Helens blew its top. Write a diary entry as if you were there that day.

Cause and Effect

Mount St. Helens erupted in 1980. "A Mountain Blows Its Top" tells some of the reasons it erupted.

When you read, think about why things happen. Why something happens is the **cause**. What happens is the **effect**.

This chart shows a cause and an effect from "A Mountain Blows Its Top."

Cause	Effect
The plates under the Cascade Range shifted.	The magma rose.

To find a cause, ask *"Why did this happen?"* To find an effect, ask *"What happened?"*

Look at this picture. Think about what is happening. Think about why it is happening. Write one sentence that tells the cause. Write another sentence that tells the effect.